THANKSGIVING

COLORING BOOKS FOR CHILDREN

AUTUMN IS HERE

SIMPLE BIG PICTURES HAPPY HOLIDAY COLORING BOOKS FOR TODDLERS AND PRESCHOOLERS

The Coloring Book Art Design Studio

THANKSGIVING
COLORING BOOKS FOR CHILDREN

by The Coloring Book Art Design Studio

THANKSGIVING
COLORING BOOKS FOR CHILDREN

THIS BOOK
BELONG TO

____

____

LET'S TEST YOUR COLOR

AUTUMN FESTIVAL
HAPPY
Thanksgiving

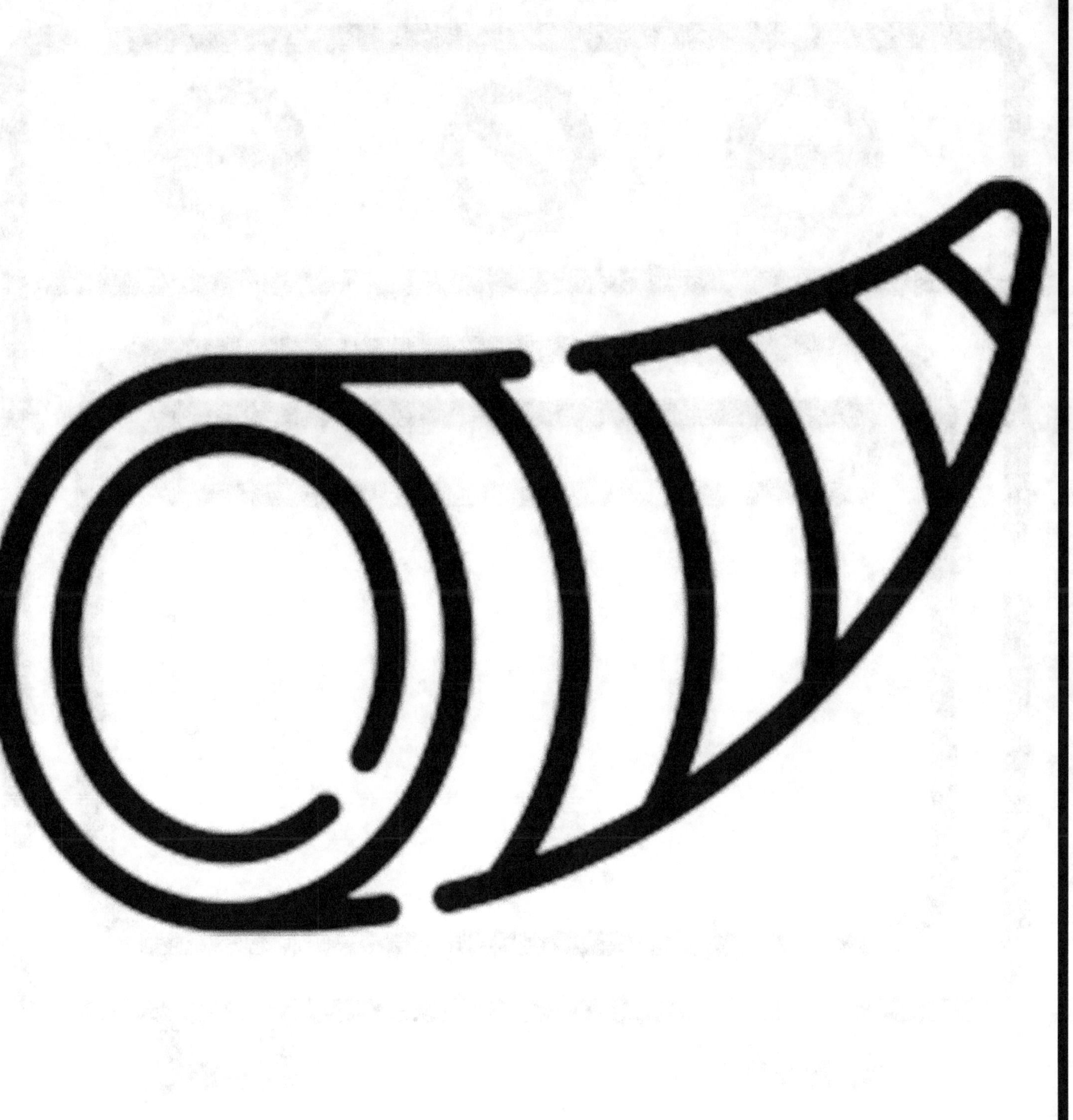

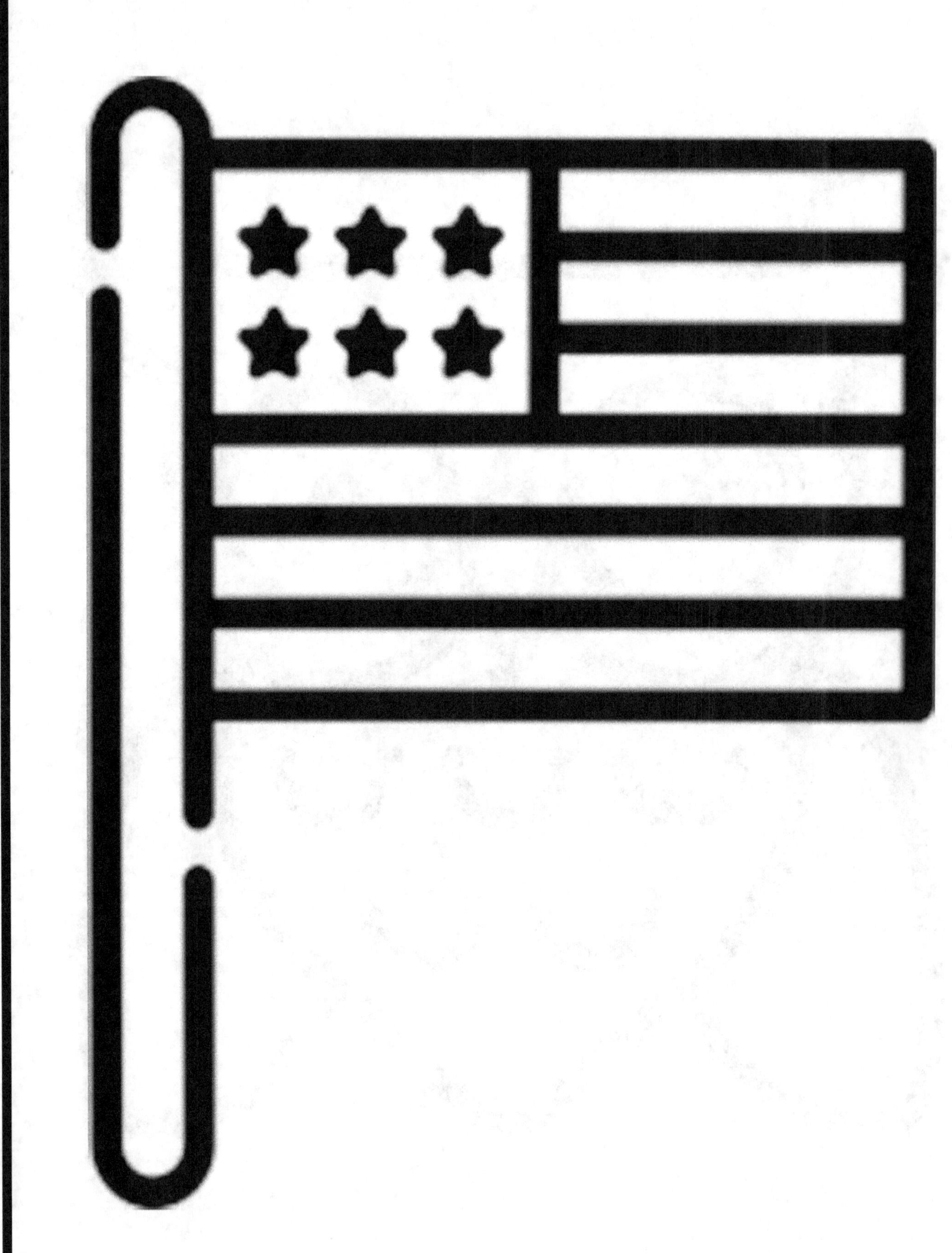

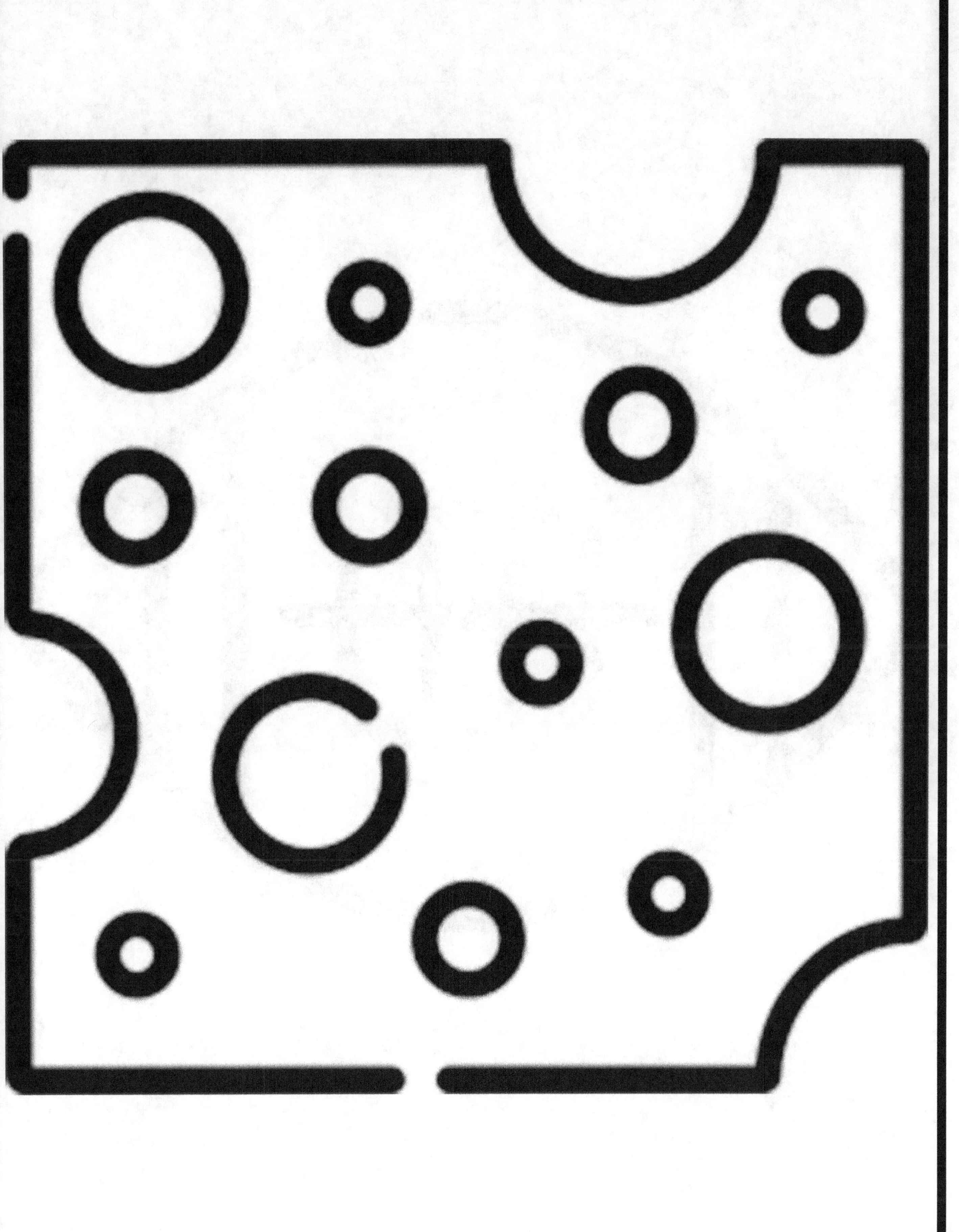

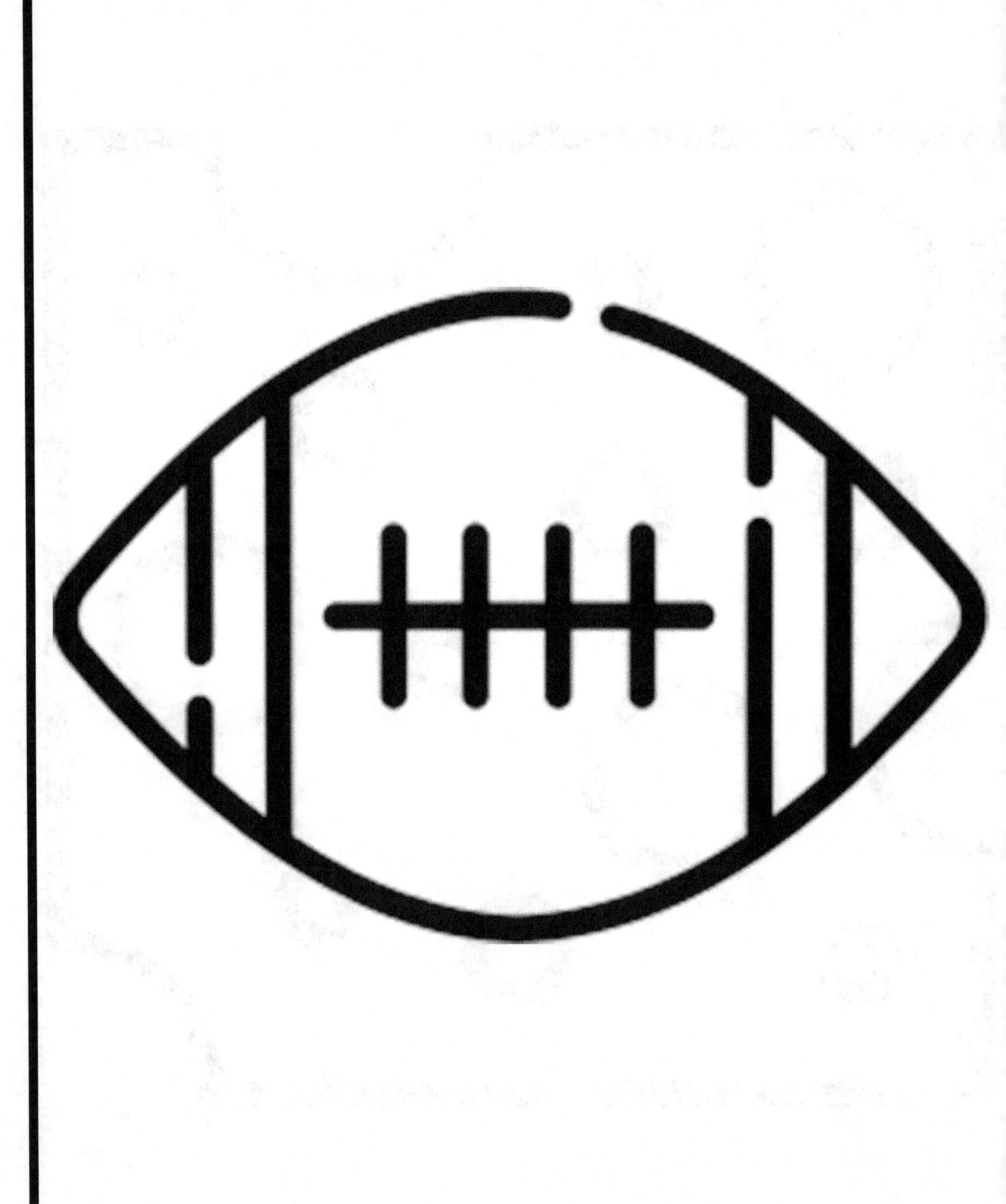

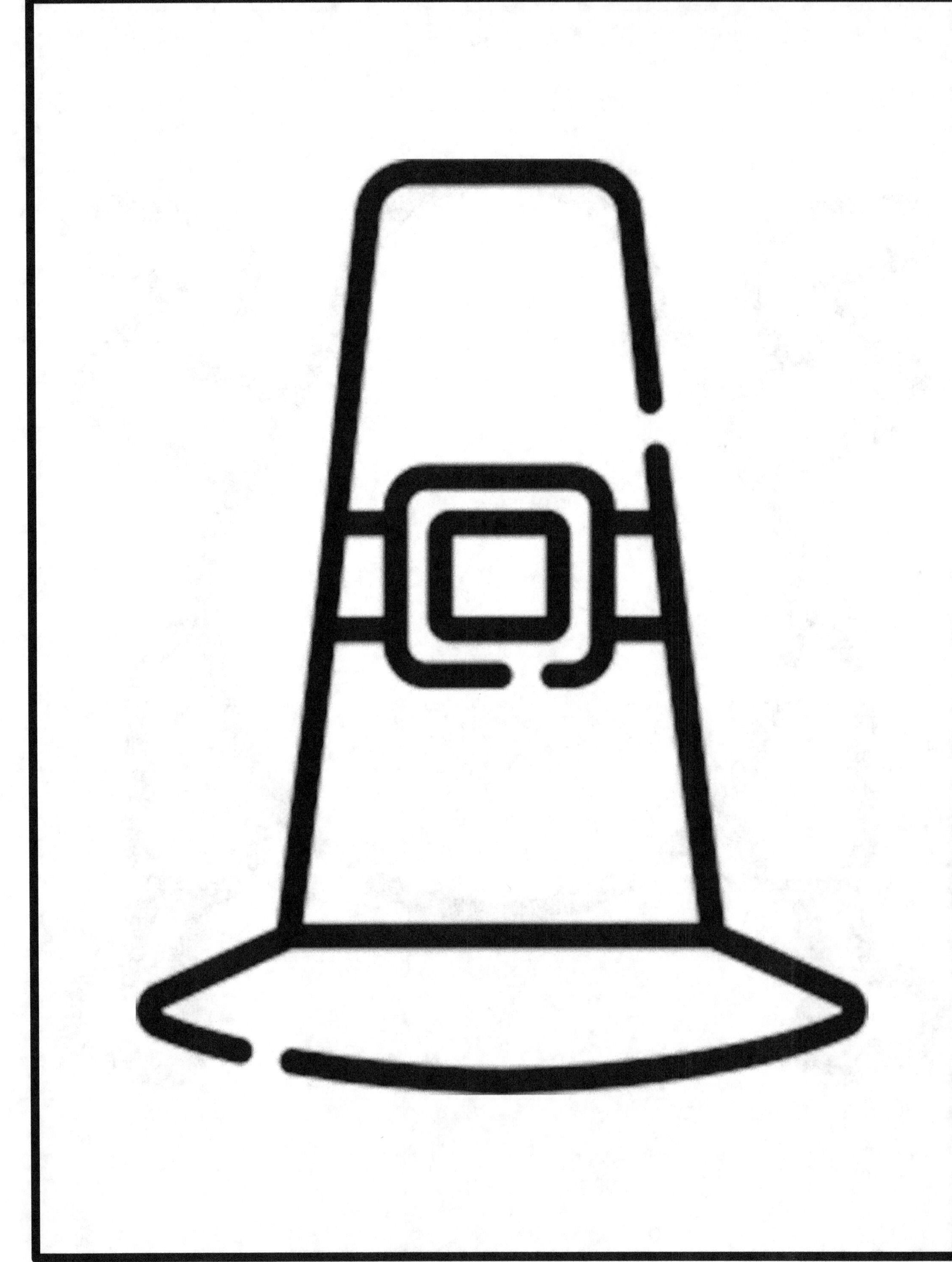

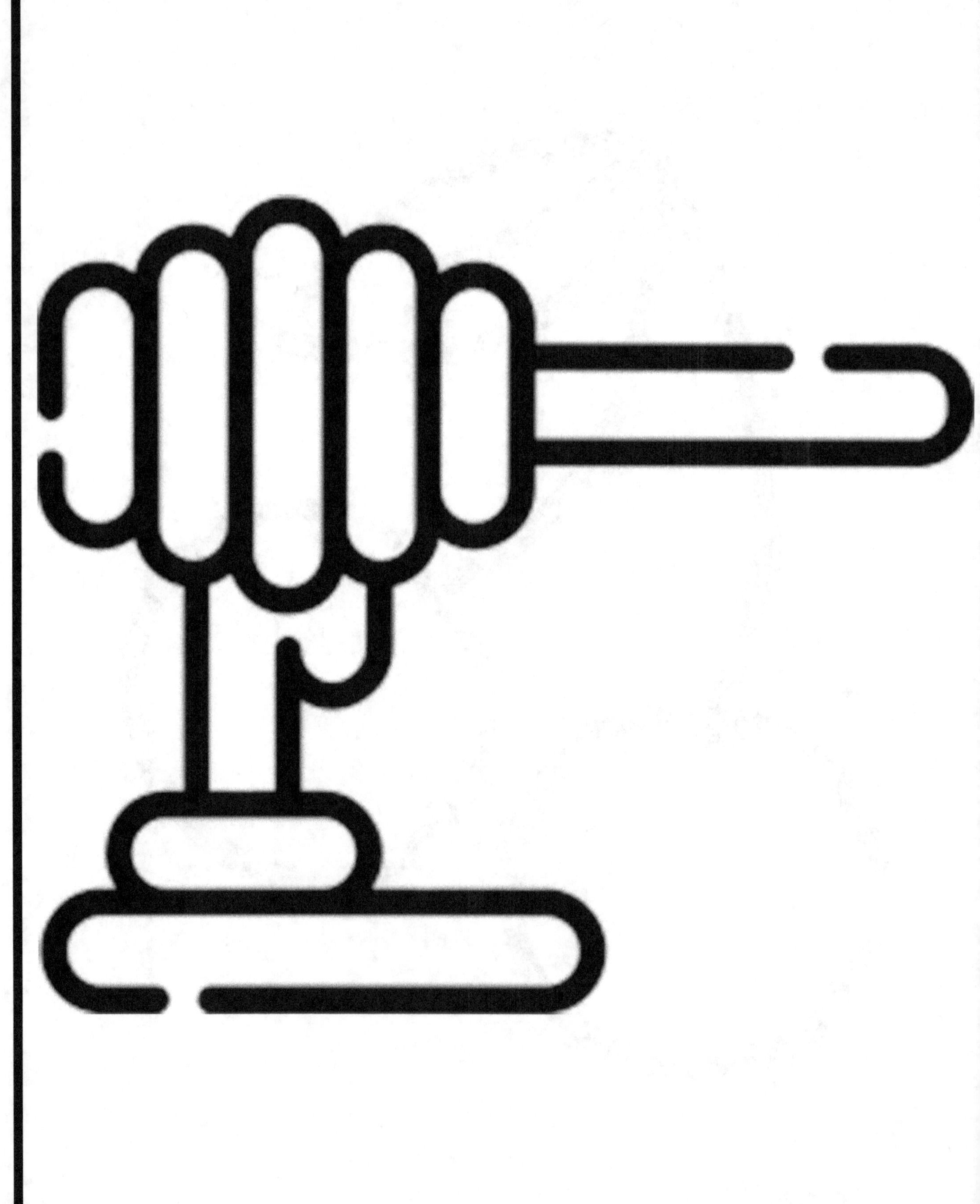

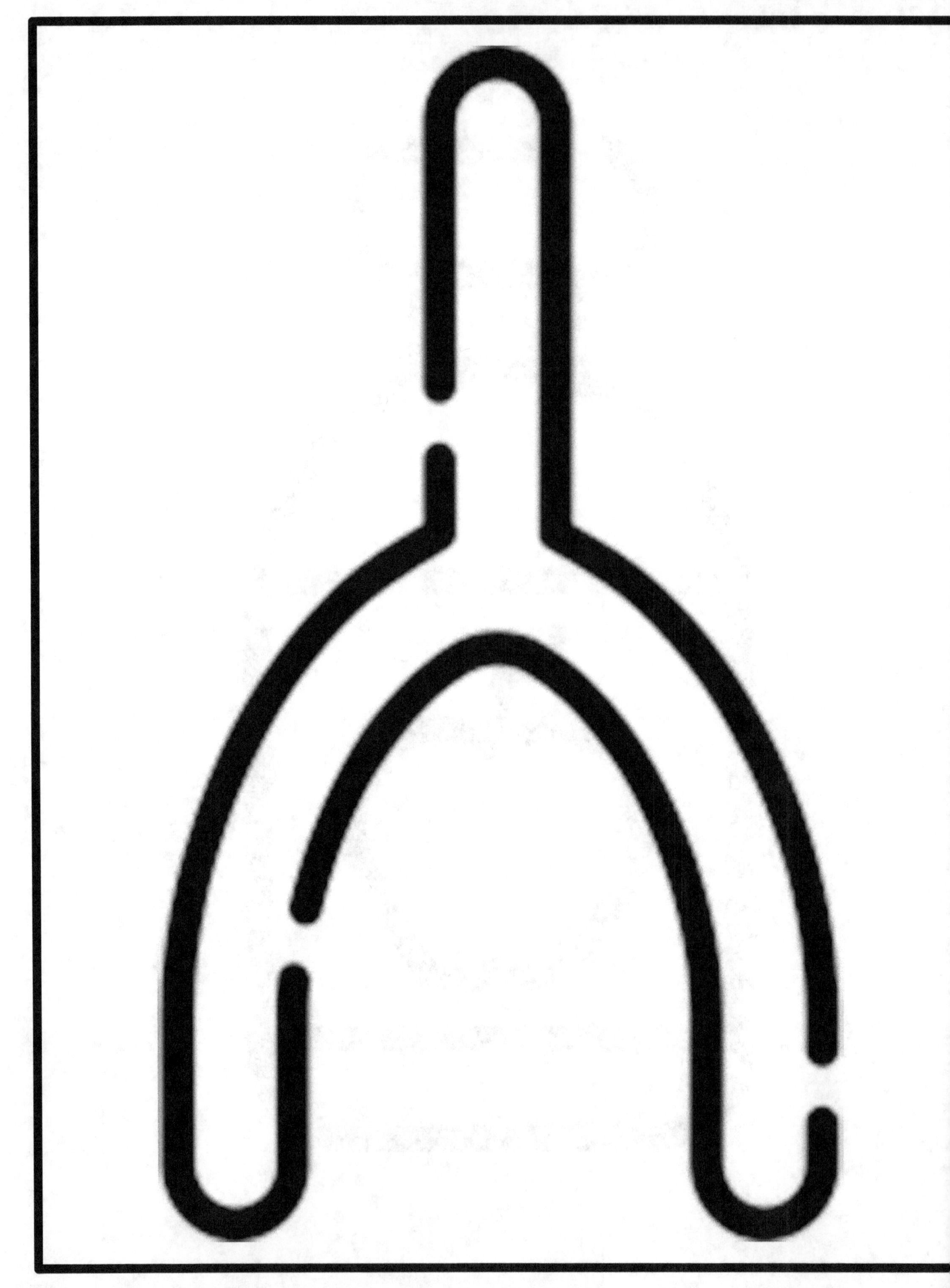

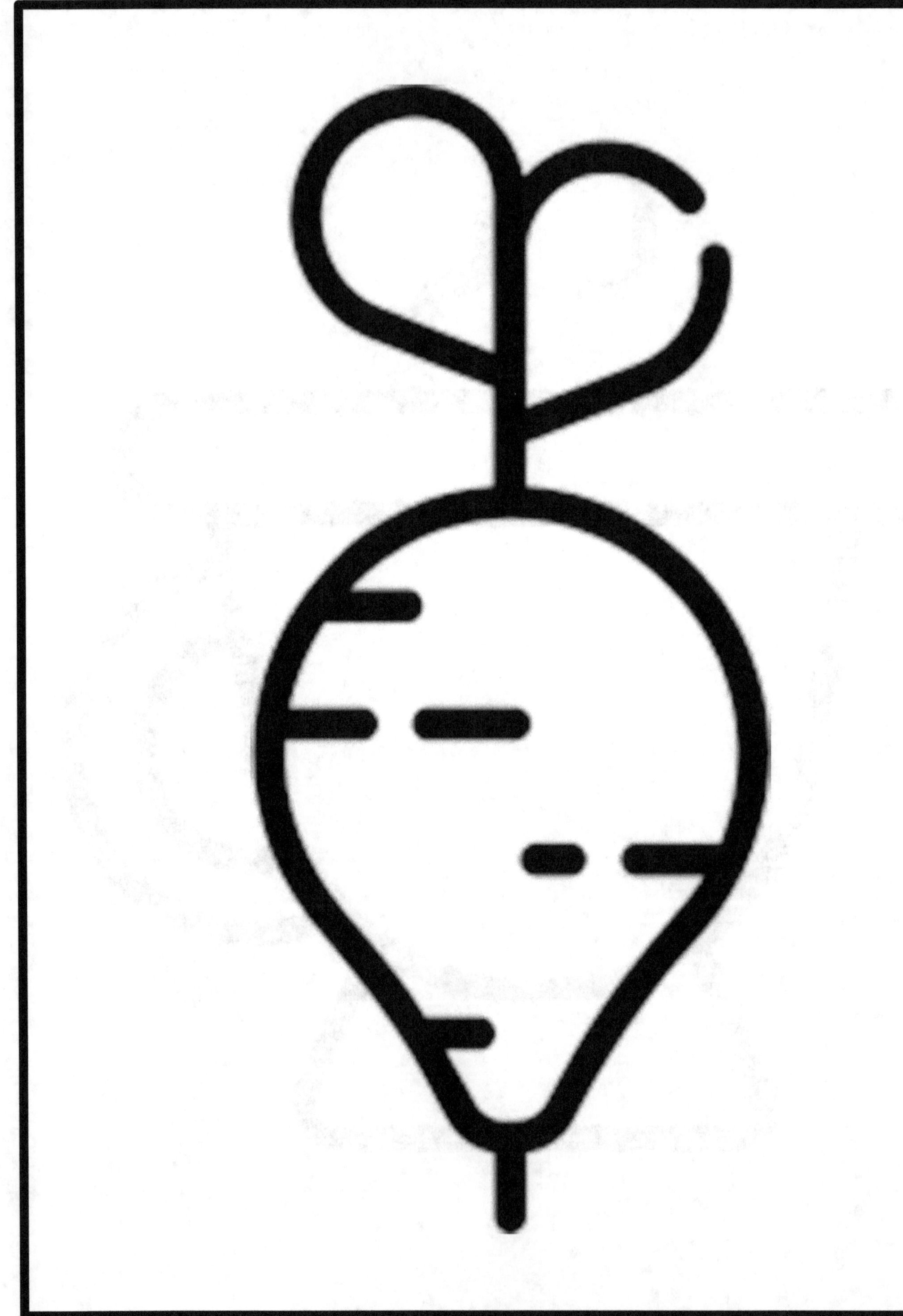

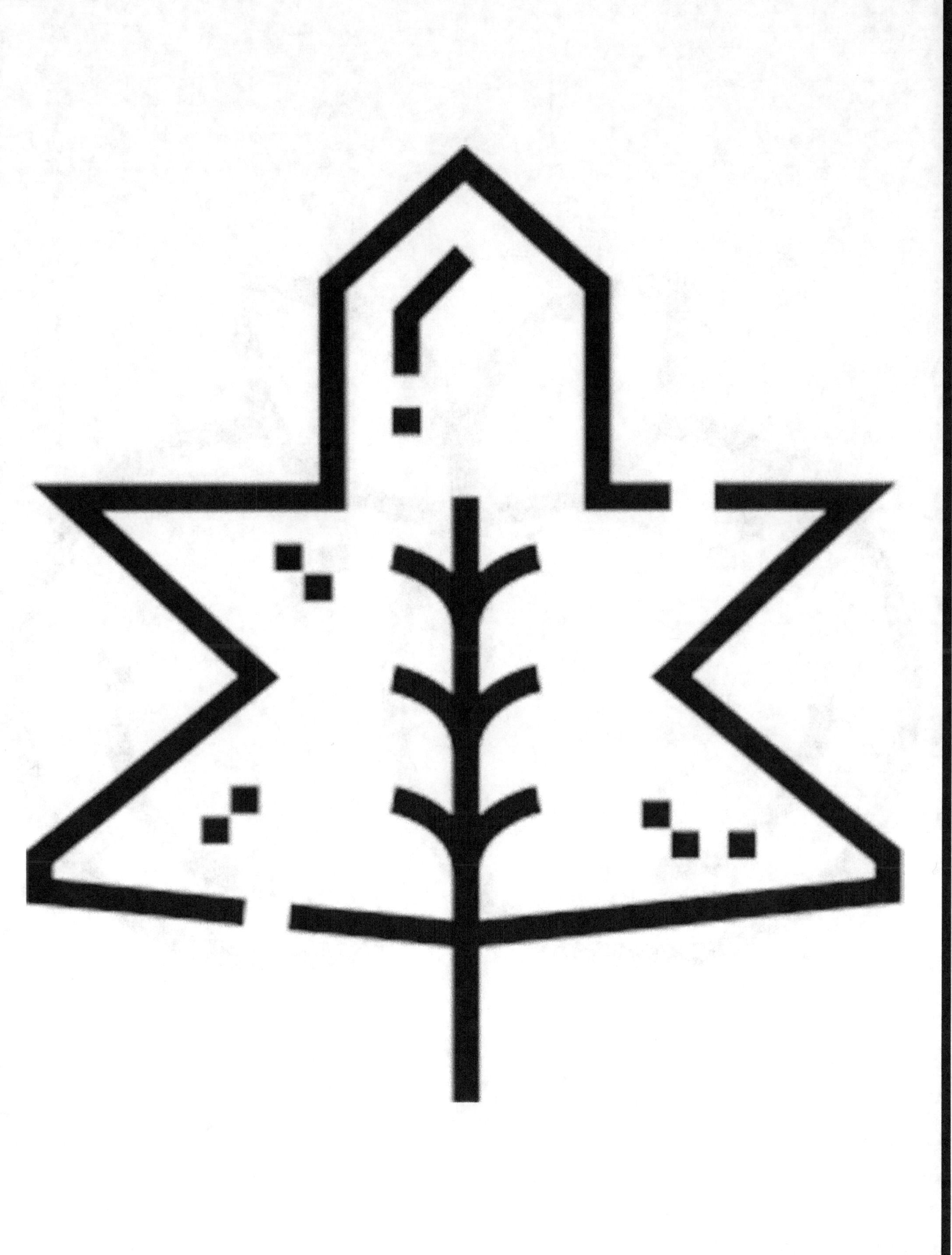

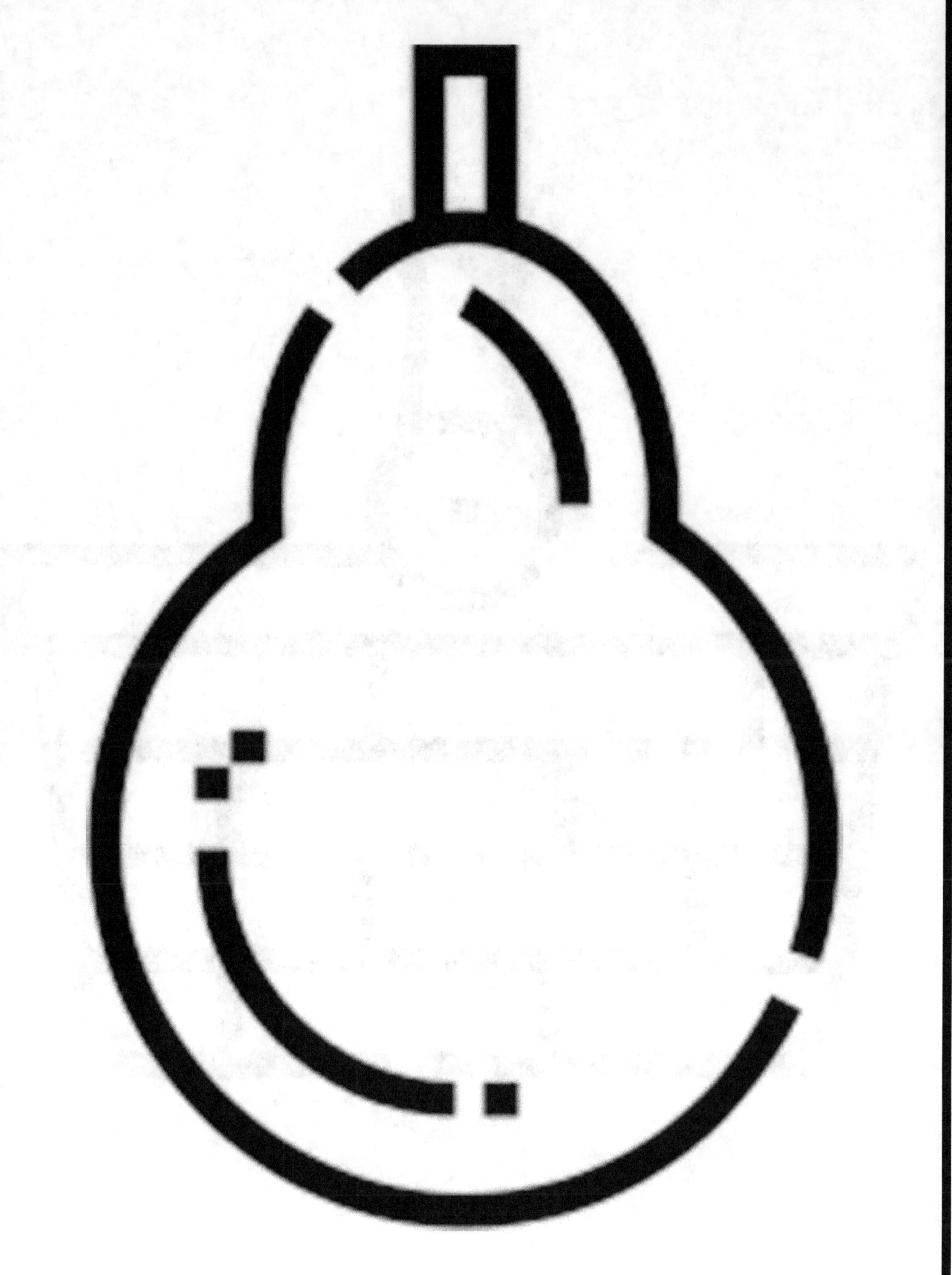

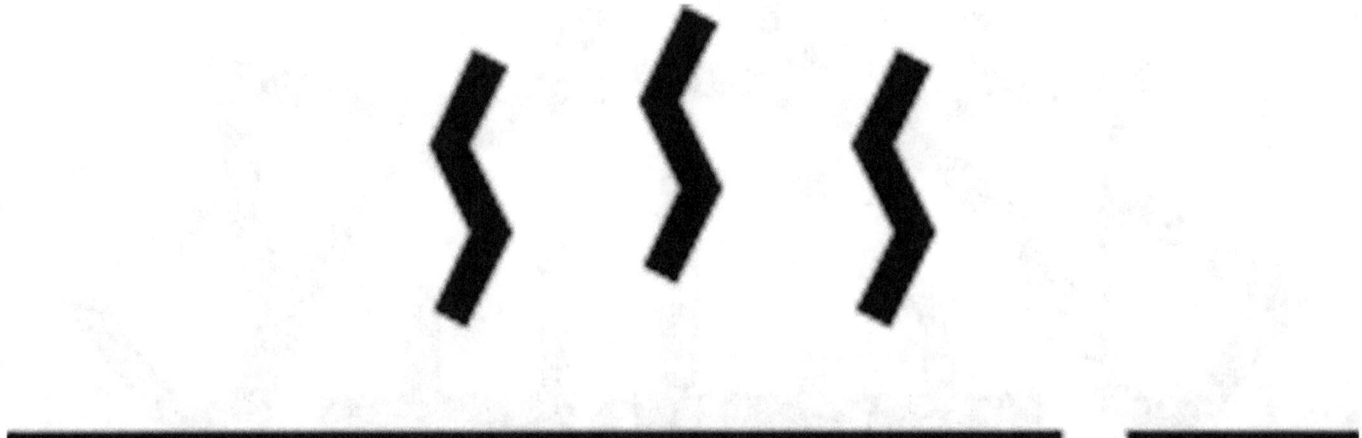

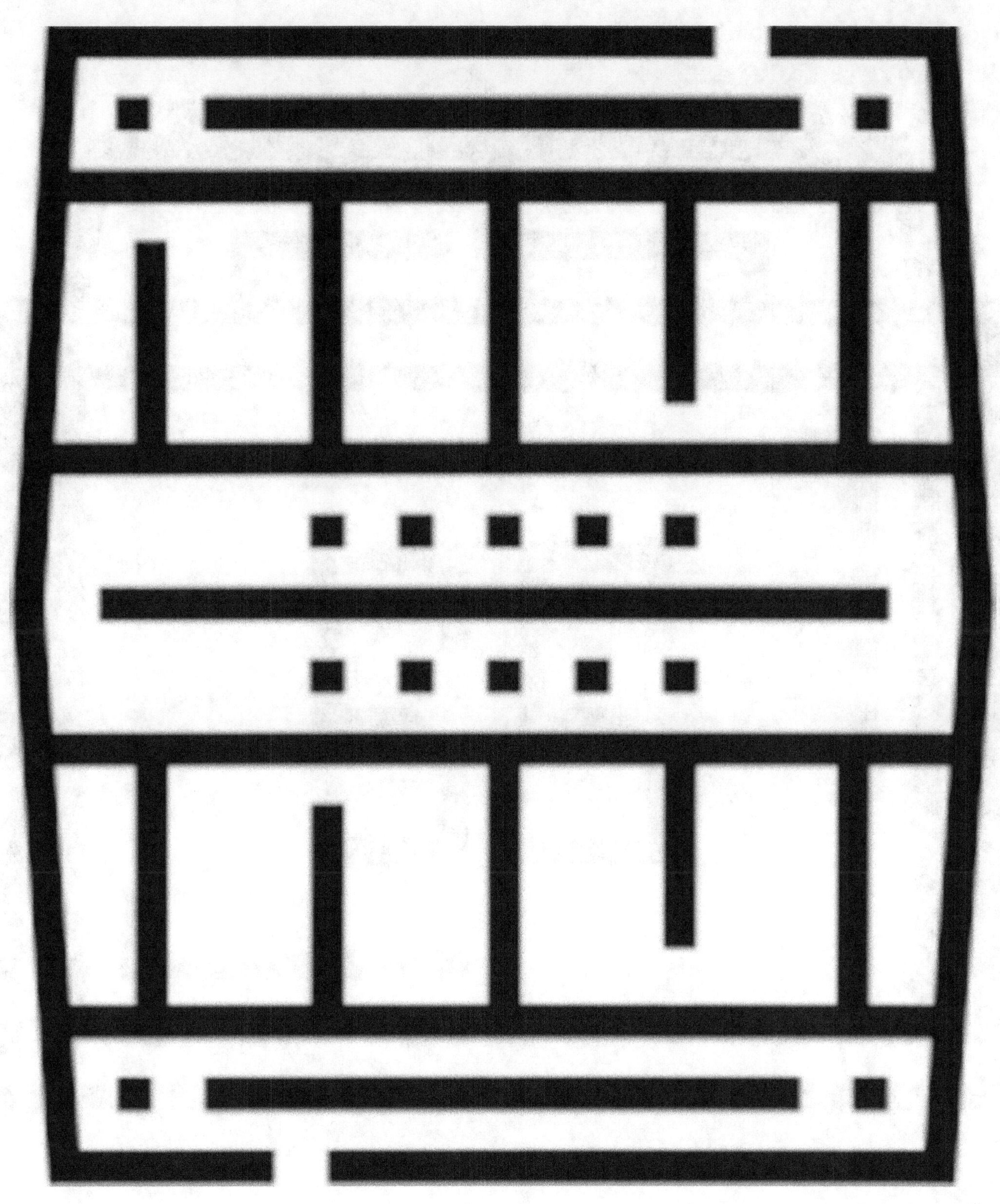

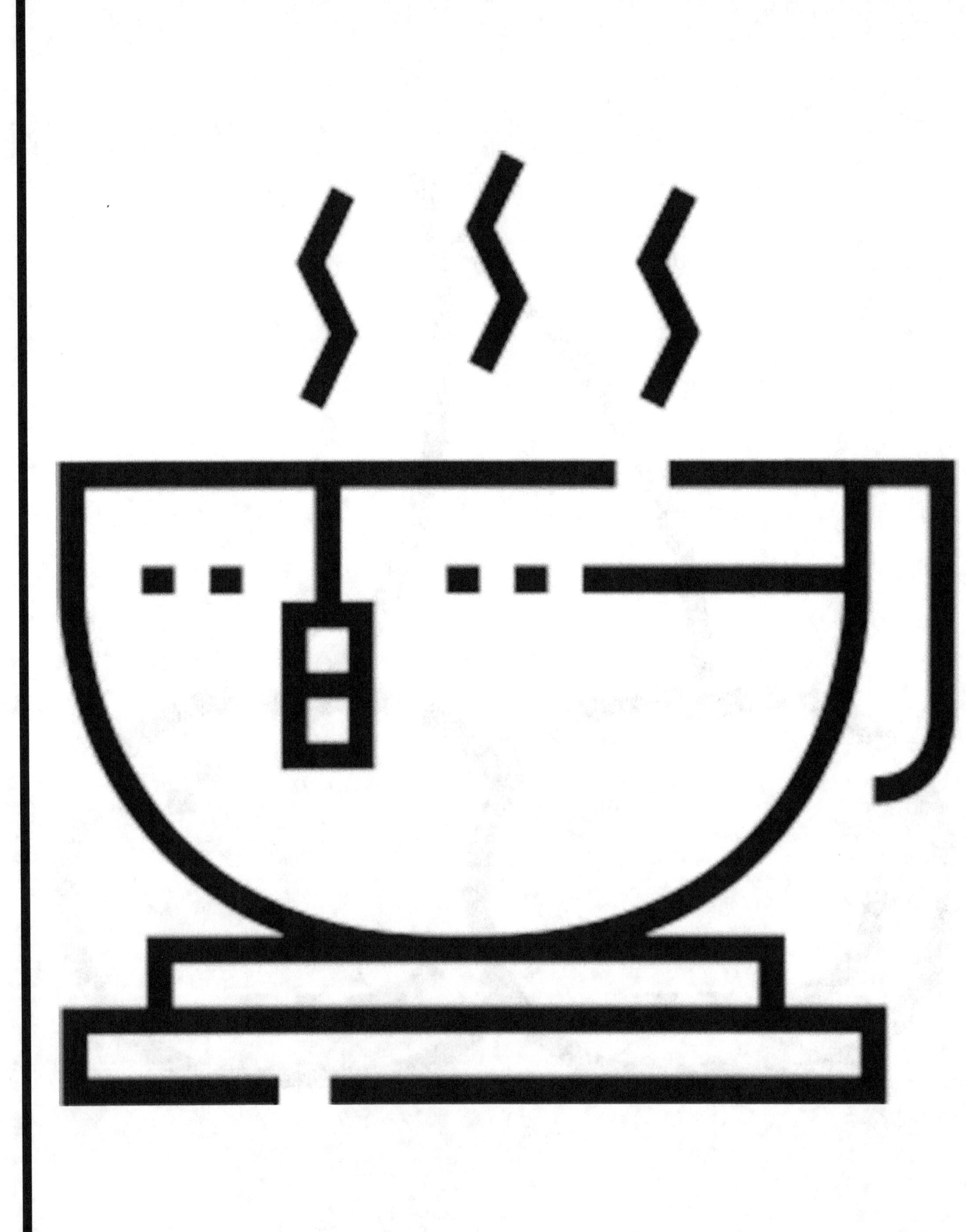

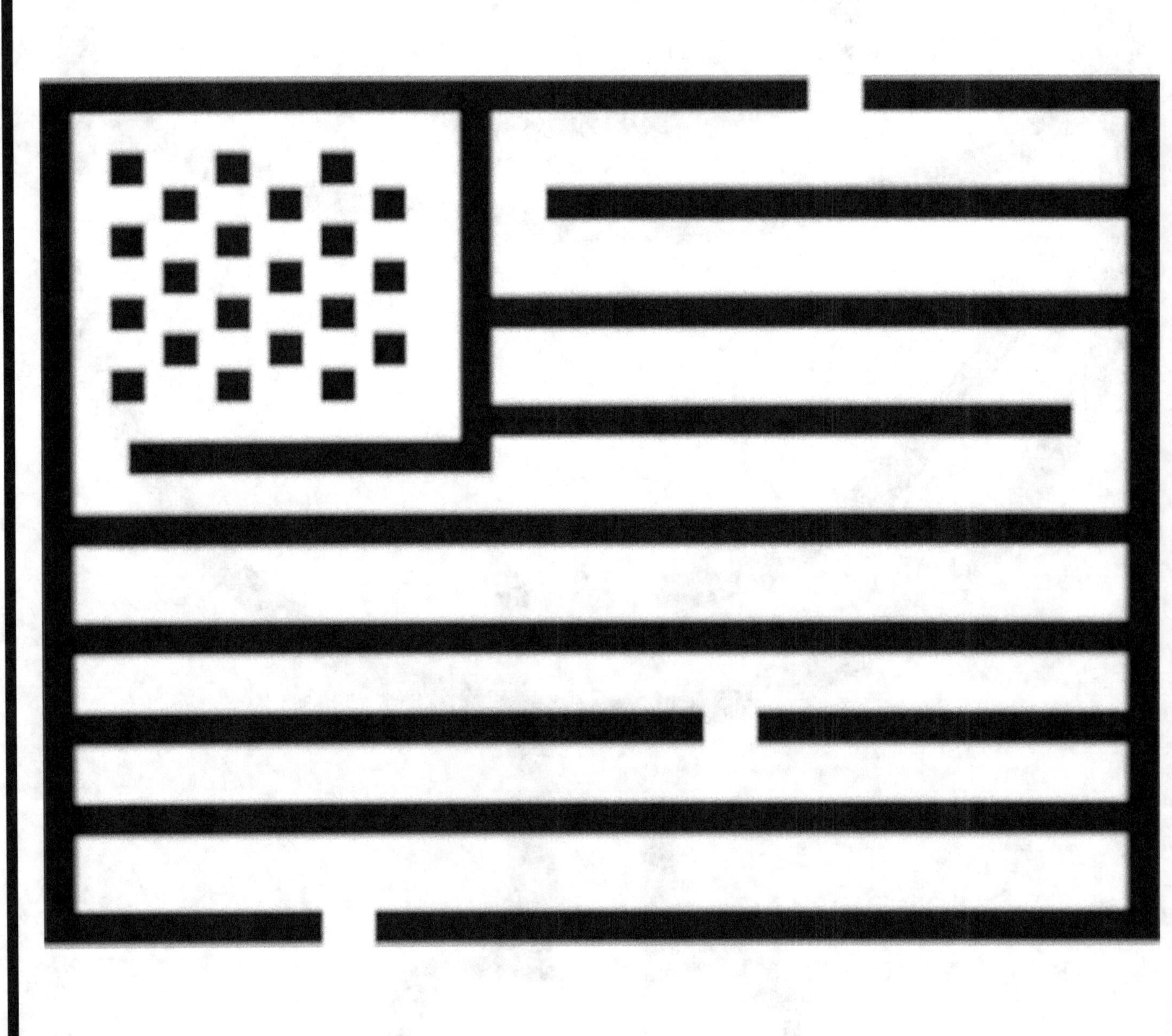

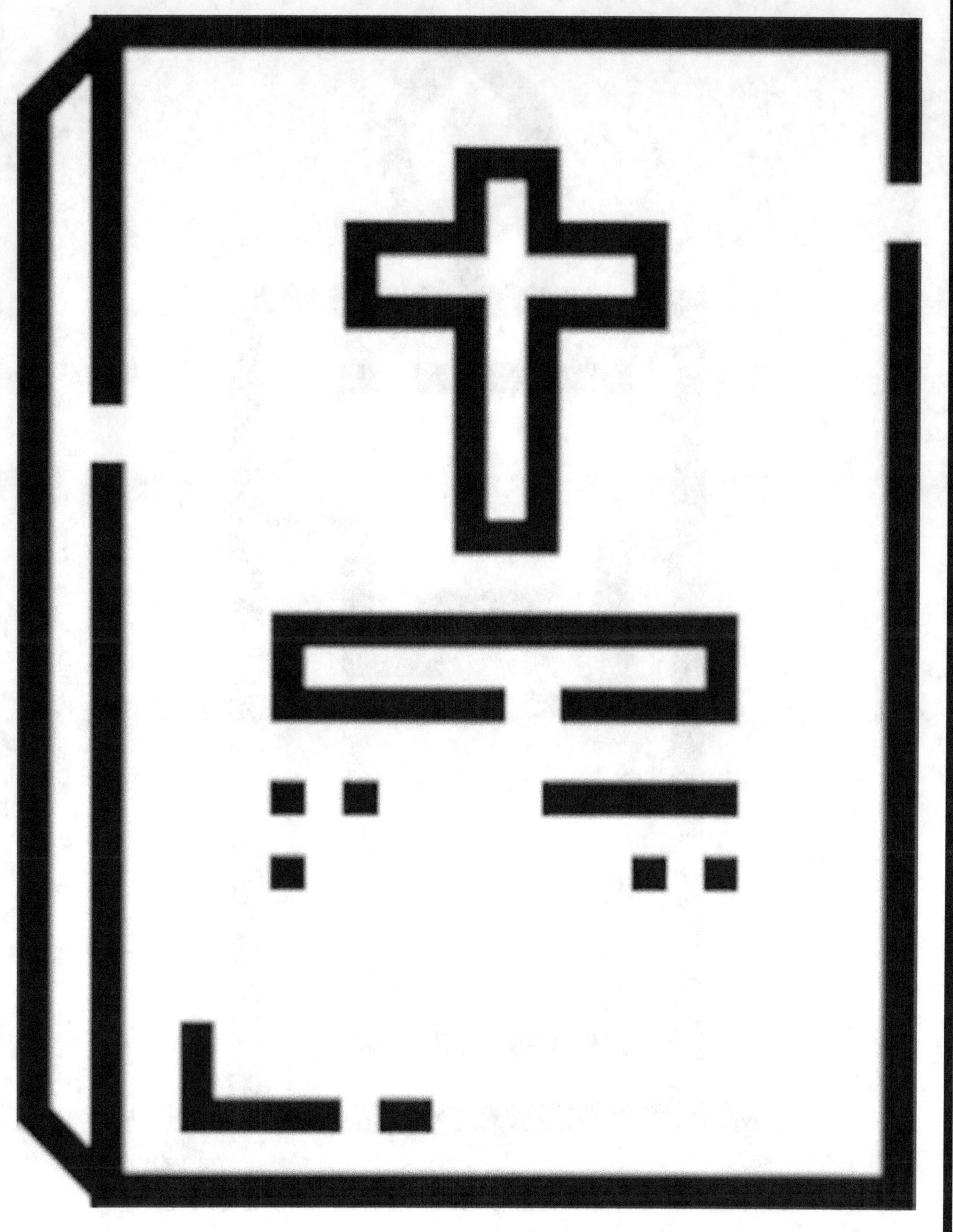

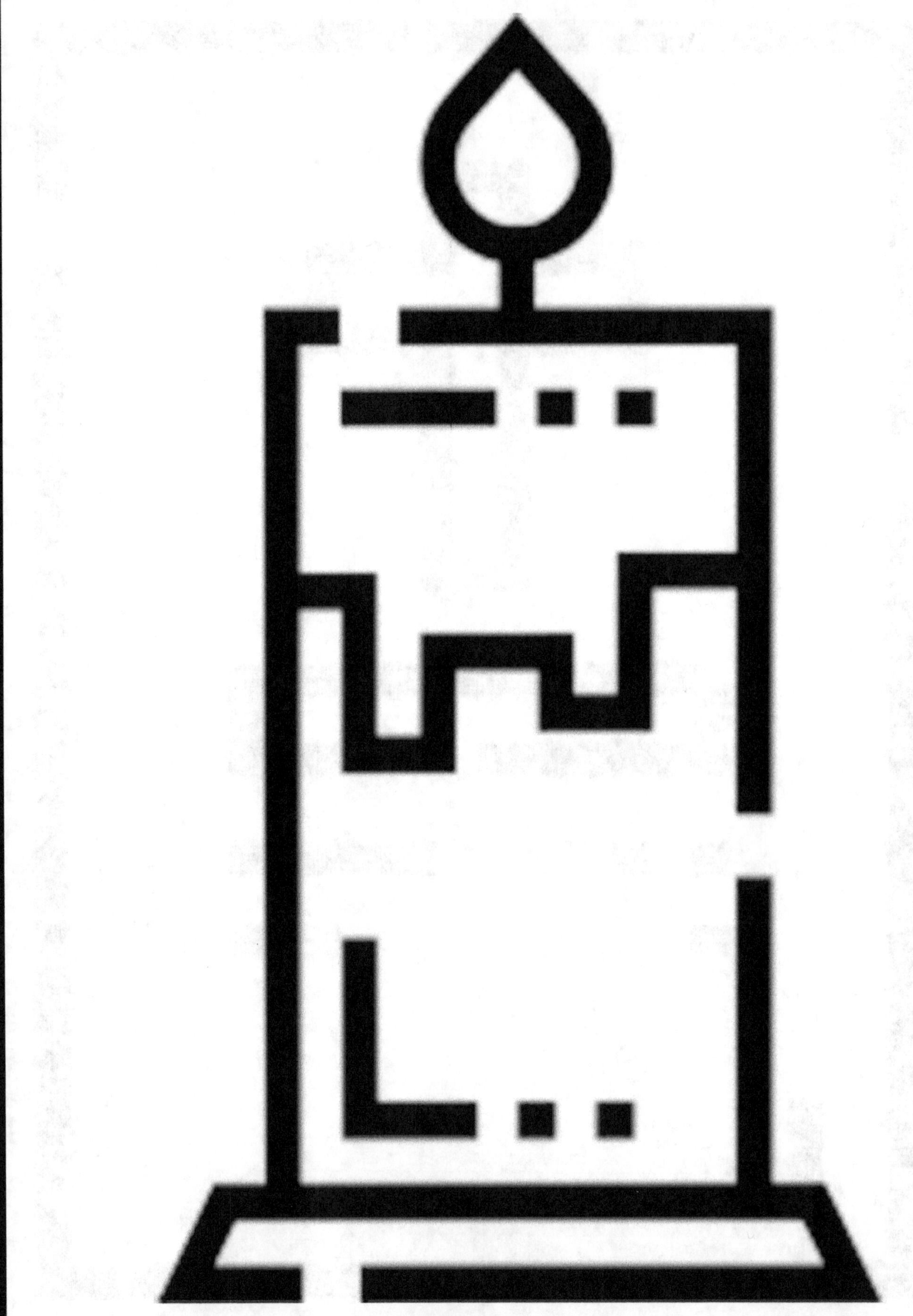

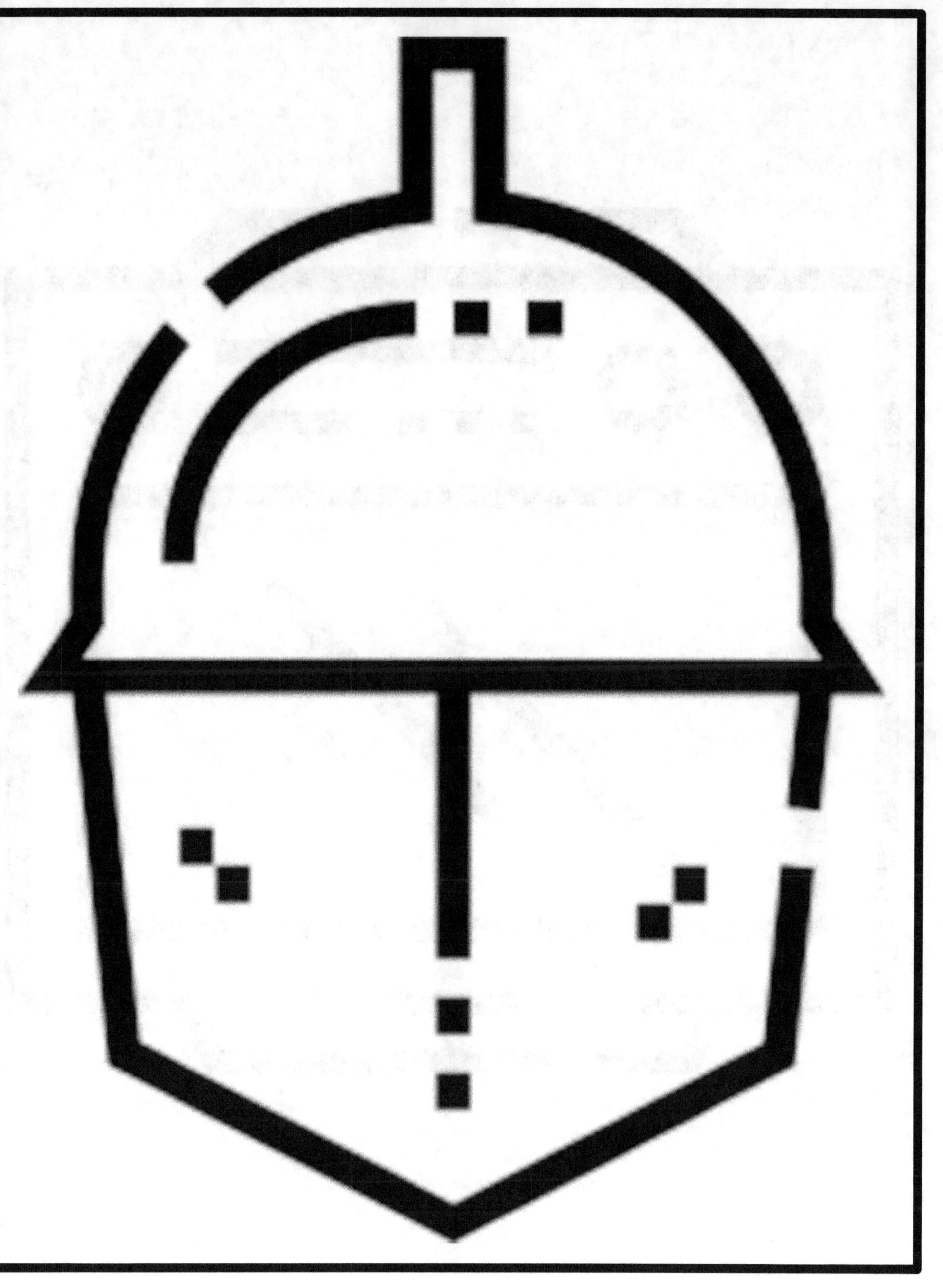

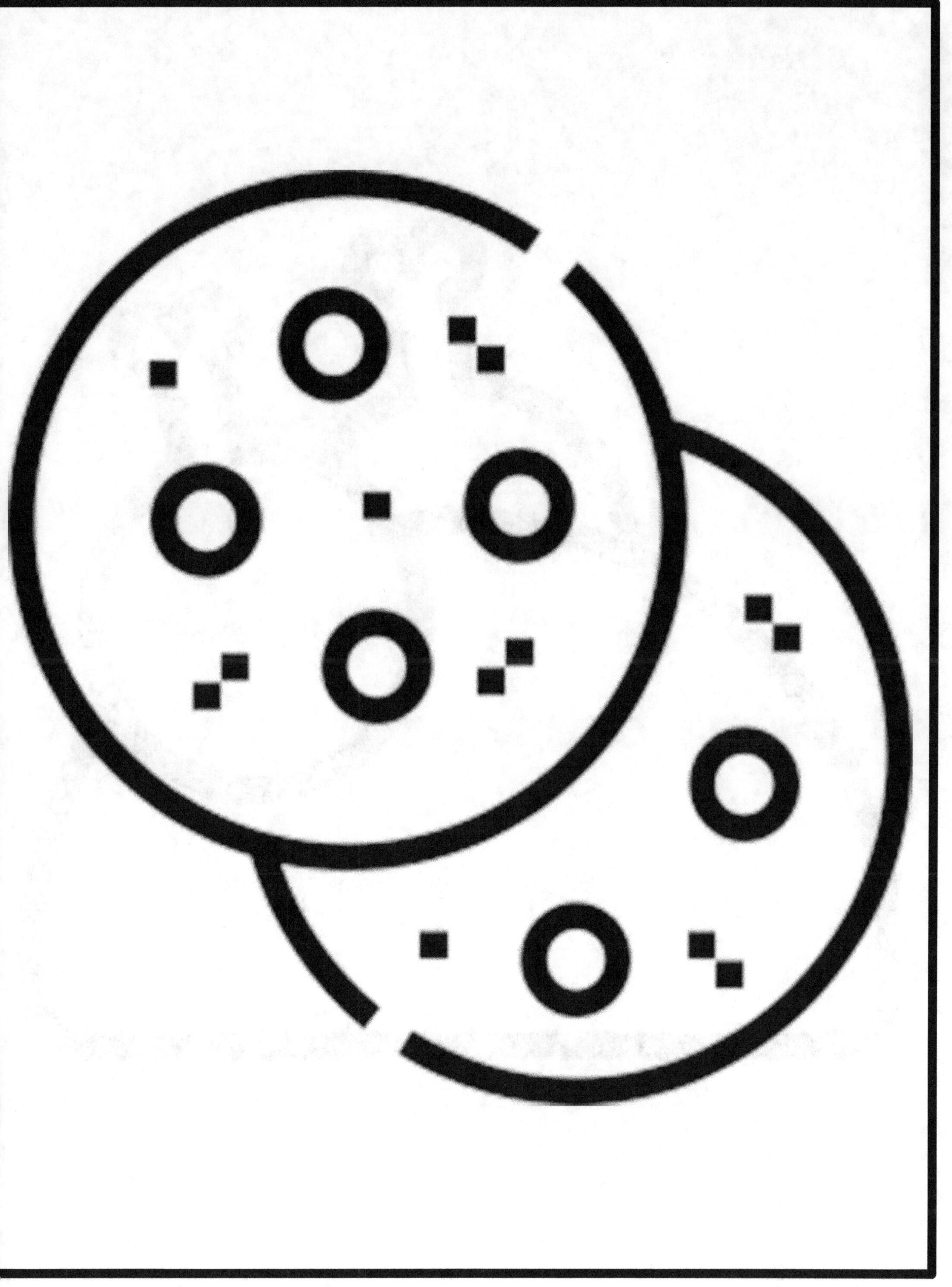

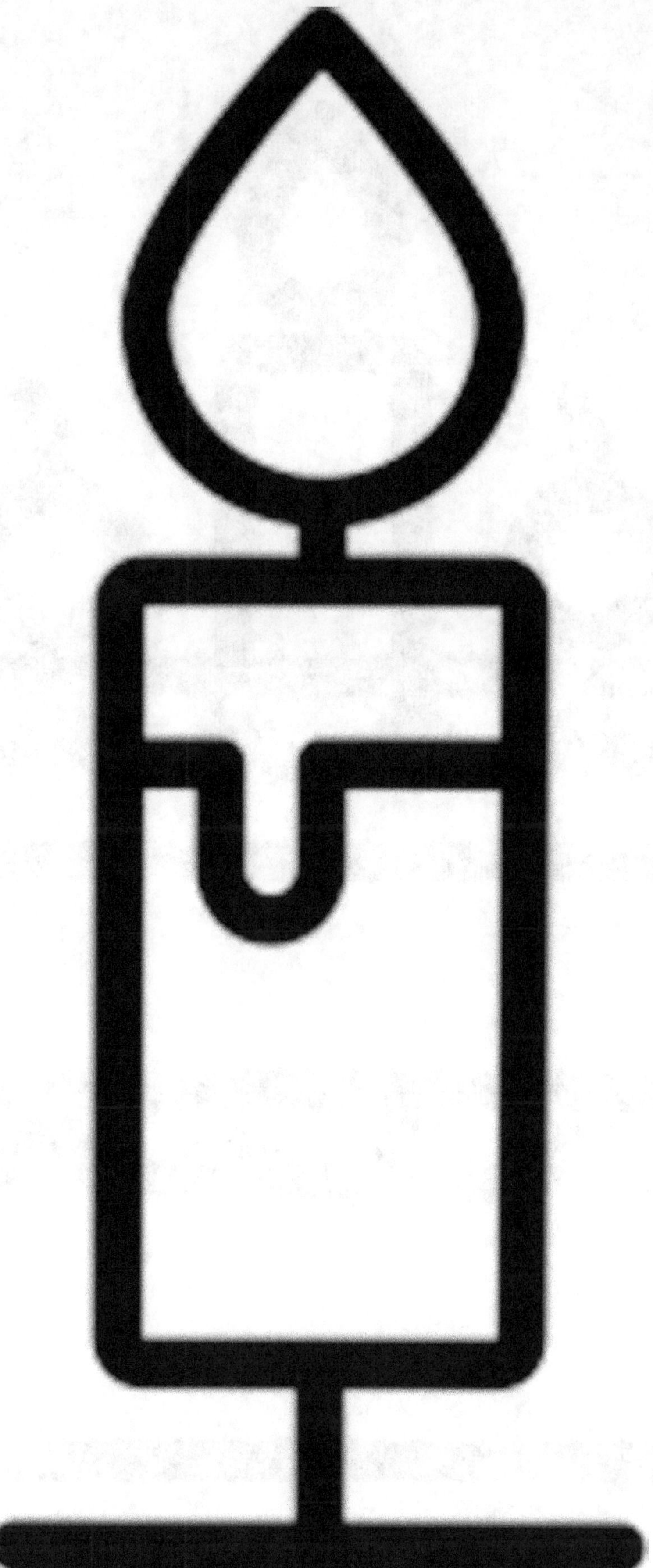

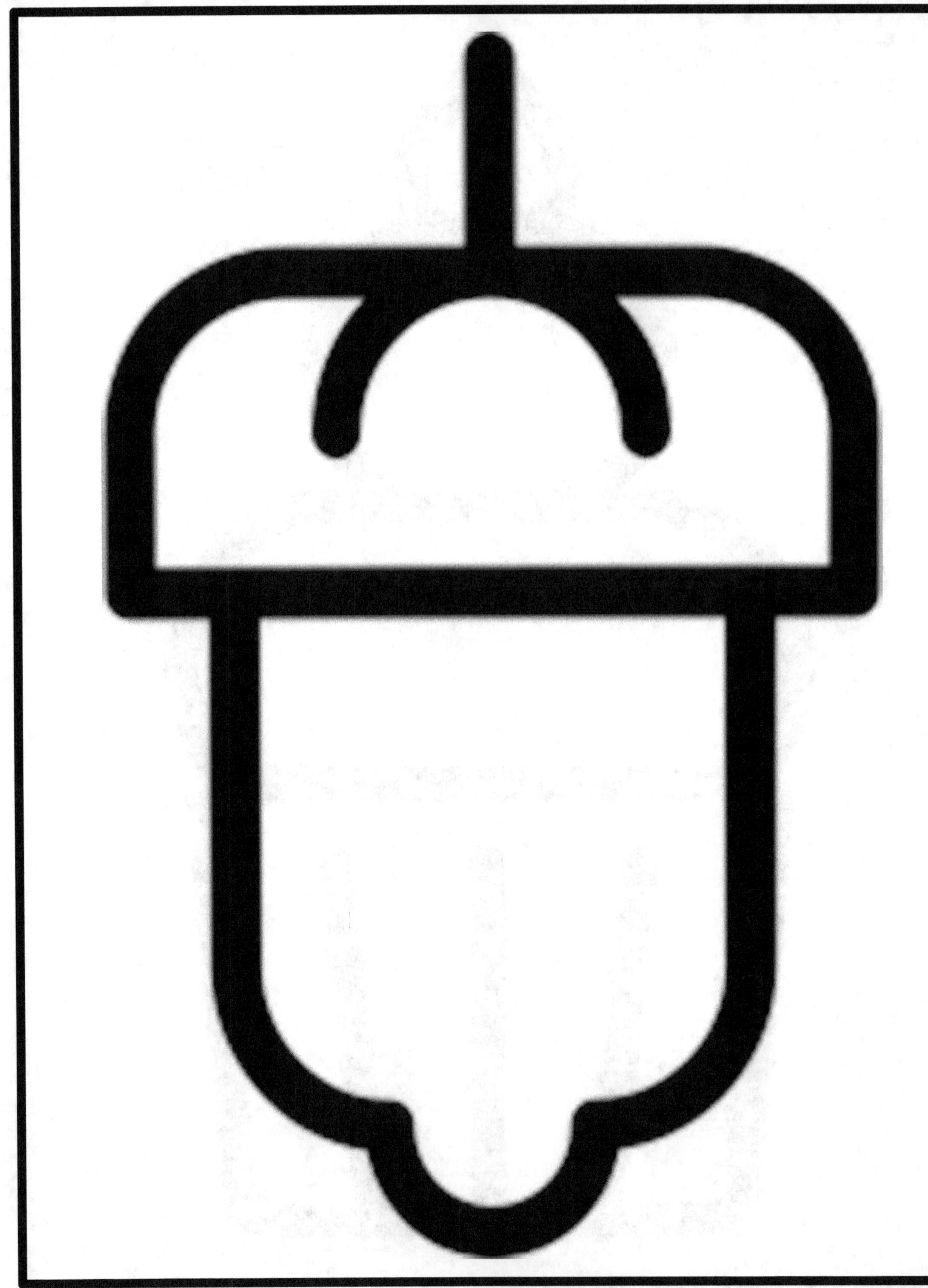

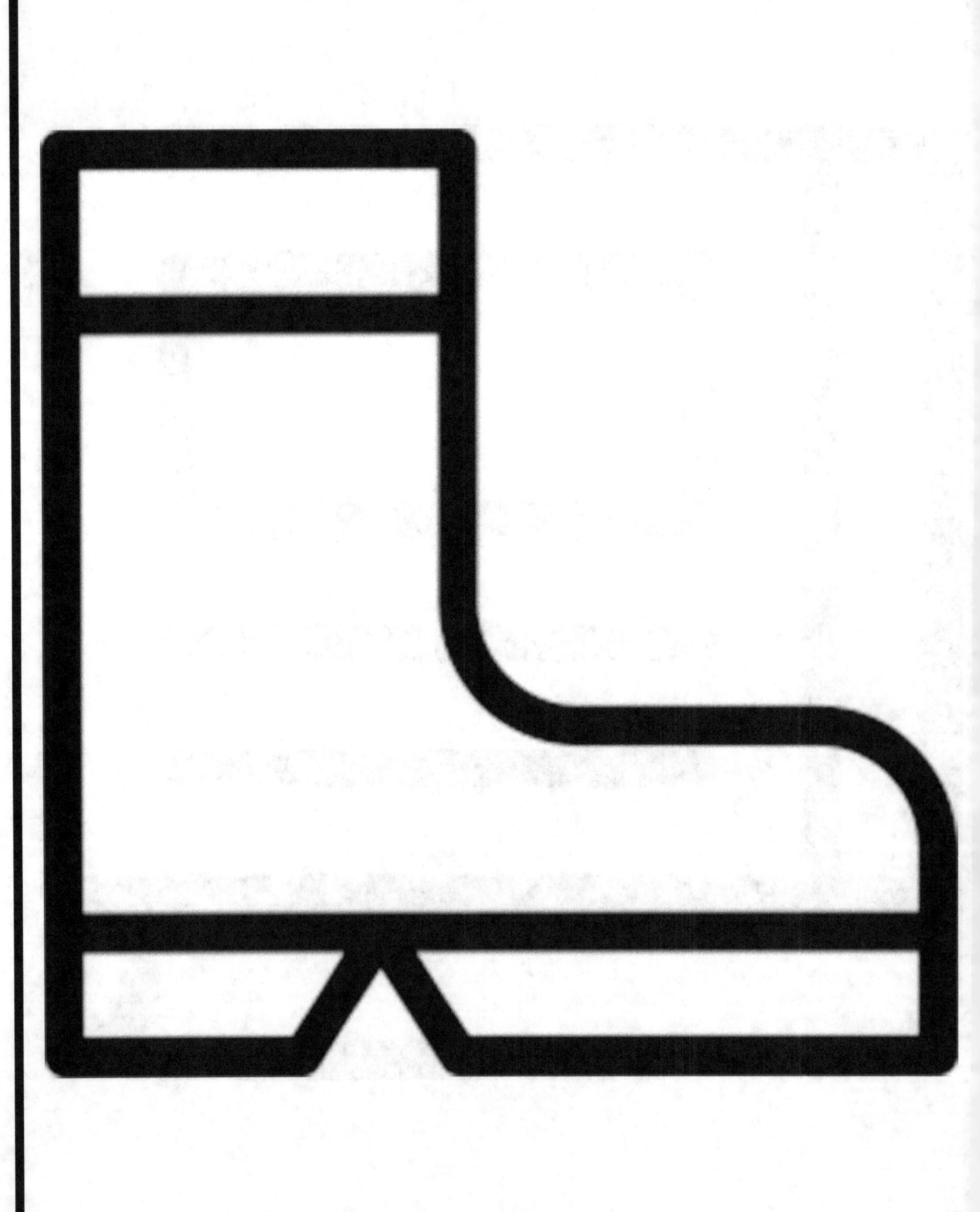

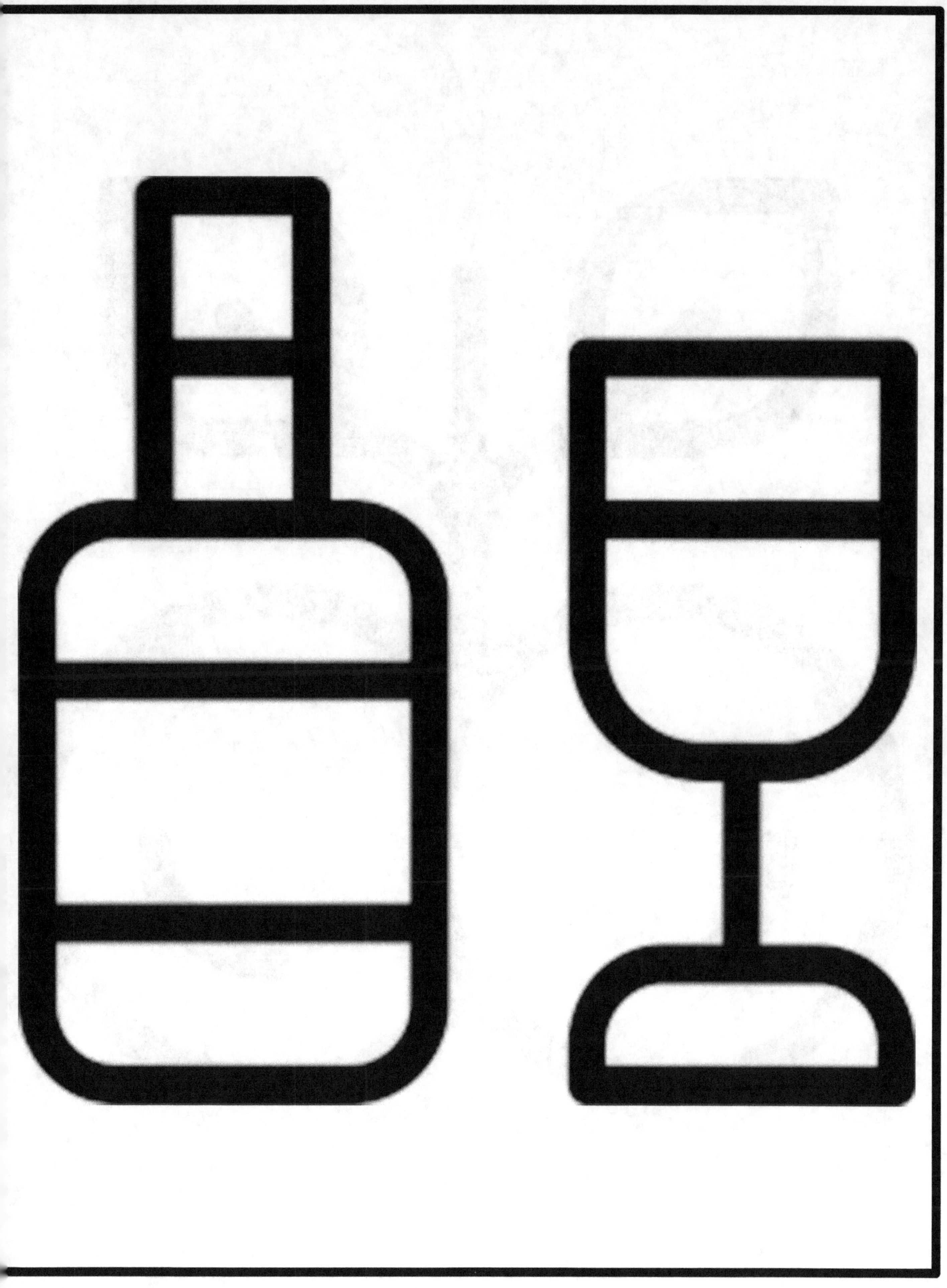

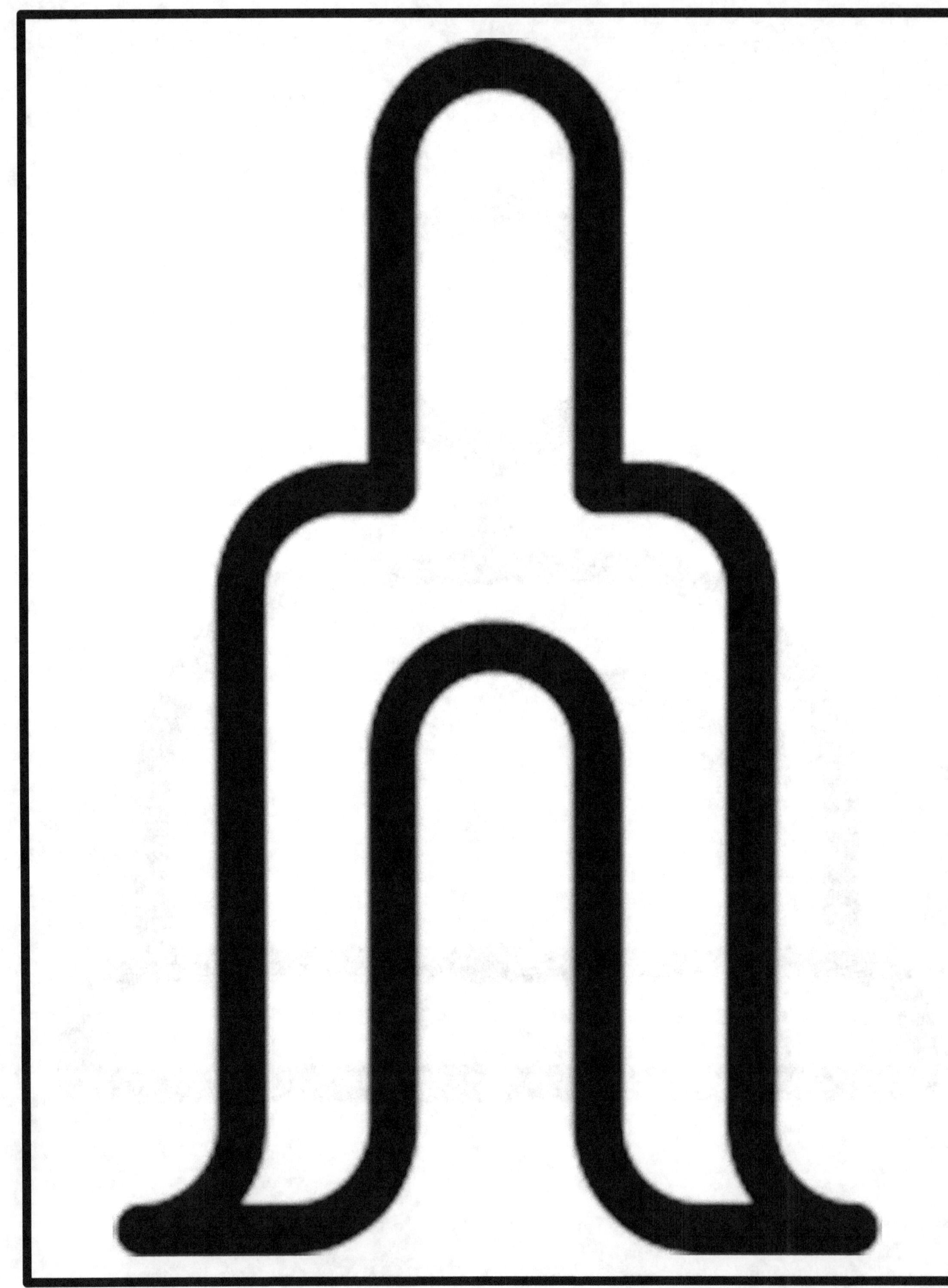

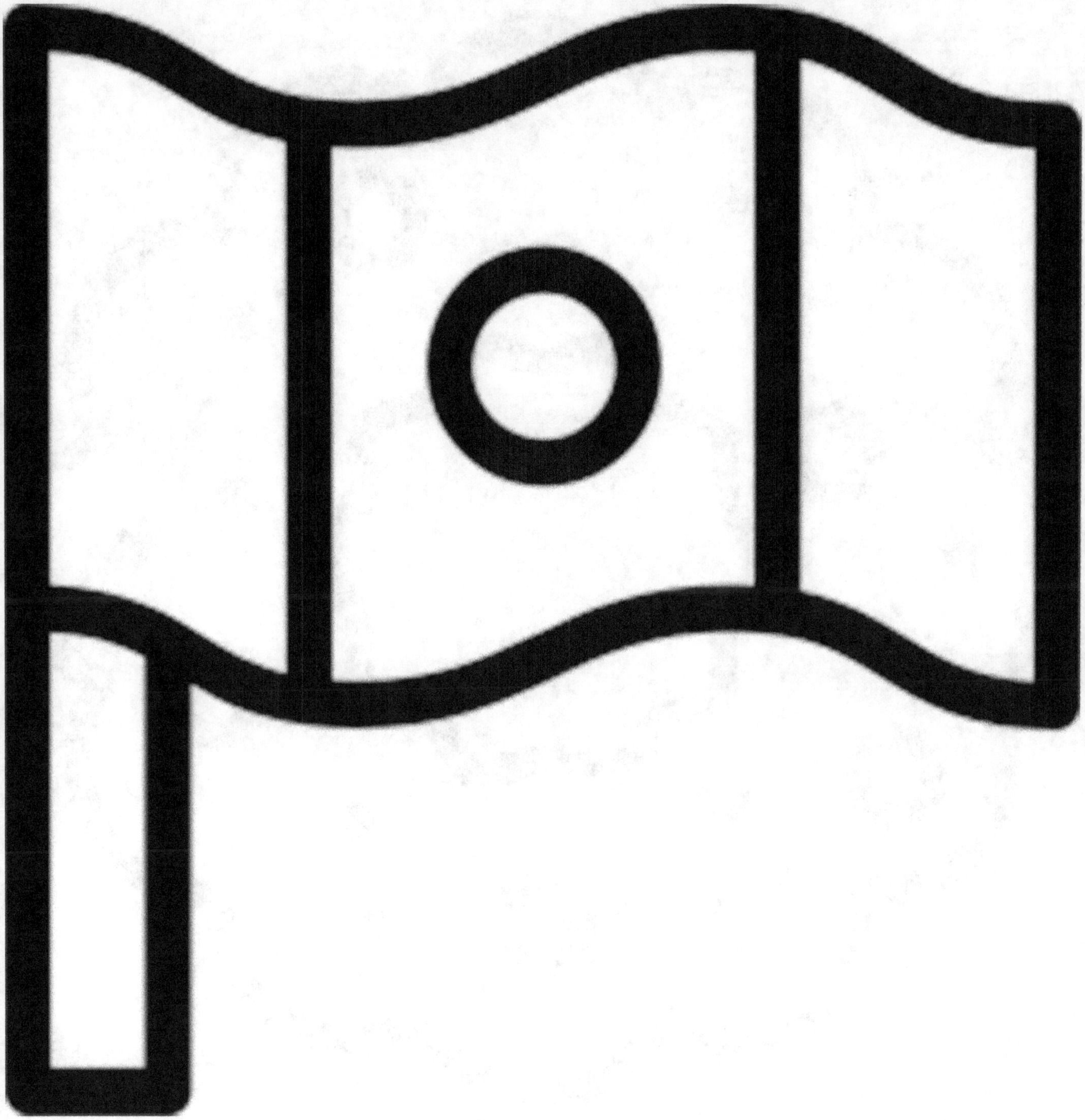

www.ingramcontent.com/pod-product-compliance
Lightning Source LLC
Chambersburg PA
CBHW081624250726
48657CB00009B/2712